this -- for you

this is for you

WRITTEN BY:
JOSSEL MANSOUR

ILLUSTRATED BY:
SAMANTHA GORGIS

TRANSLATED BY:
SAWSAN SHAKIR

THIS IS FOR YOU
Copyright © 2017 Jossel Mansour

ISBN-10: 1546390227
ISBN-13: 978-1546390220

⋮

my name is jossel, pronounced jih.zel. growing up as a child i allowed others to say or spell my name in whichever way they would like. it took me 22 years of age to correct people who were still spelling or mispronouncing my name. my mother and father were both born and raised in baghdad, iraq. they were labeled as immigrants as soon as they stepped foot on american land. they did not understand or speak the english language. it wasn't until i started working on this book that i realized how hard it must have been for my parents to start a new life here. not knowing the language. not having the resources to learn the language. they only knew arabic and aramaic, the languages they spoke back home and still do until this day. luckily, i was taught how to speak aramaic at a young age. aramaic is also known as chaldean, which is the language jesus christ spoke. sadly, i believe the aramaic language is slowly dying. it is nearly impossible to try and find someone who can still read or write in the aramaic language. i will forever be grateful for knowing how to speak it. i did, however, always find it beautiful. the way the english language is written from left to right, while the arabic language is written from right to left. art, for me- isn't only drawings and paintings. art is language. art is the way we speak. art is our native tongue. throughout this book you will find each piece written in english and only a few translated into arabic. please know, when it comes to translating there are different dialects and i chose the dialect which is more well-known. each piece was translated with words i thought fit best. i felt it was only right to provide my parents and many others with a book, which wouldn't be too much of a struggle to read *for the first time.*

in 2015 i picked up a journal and pen. i wrote about how my days went and what i was feeling. some days i filled up 6 pages' front to back and other days i did not want to touch my journal. i always admired poetry and if someone were to ask me who my favorite poets were i would list them immediately. i came across a woman named margarite camaj one day. and wow. if only i could explain the emotions i felt when reading her work. that day, i knew i wanted to write poetry. i knew that i too, wanted to make people feel. so, i tried. i tried too hard. i ended up with two very well written poems and that was it. *trying* to write didn't sit right with me. i stopped. i did not want to force words together. i did not want to force poetry. i put my journal away for months. until the day i met him. i didn't even have to try to write a poem, the words came to me as if i've known poetry my entire life. freely. a painting poured out of me with colors i did not even know existed. and here it is. all in this book. it's crazy huh? how one person can impact your life in such a short amount of time. how this one person can start a spark in you. i know that many of you reading this have met someone in your life who has started a spark in you. and only a spark. they tend to leave before a fire starts. whatever their reasoning might be. i am here to tell you that it is solely up to you to choose what to do with this spark they have started in you. do you let it die out because they have left? or do you allow it start a fire within you on your own? if you are wondering, i took this spark and i placed it somewhere i knew would never cause it to die out. *my heart*. every. single. day. a fire burns inside of me and i don't have to worry if the flames will be extinguished one day. because i decide that. only me. no one else. i can only hope that you choose to be the only one who can decide that too.

to god,

thank you. for everything.

إلى الله ،

شكرا لك. لكل شيء .

to my mother-
mama, ever since i was a little girl i was able to see all of the pain you once bared inside your eyes. until this day, i still run to you to see if you're okay when i hear your cry. & you continue to do the same for me. thank you mama, for always being there for me. i love you.

to my father-
bab, there is one memory of you & i that i could never forget. we were in the car, driving. there was a moment during our car ride where i started laughing. you looked at me and said- *whenever i hear your laugh, it is always filled with so much life. please, always continue to laugh like this because there aren't many moments in our life in which we get to.* thank you bab, for always reminding me of what happiness should be. i love you.

to evette-
thank you, for being the older sister i never had. you have stood by my side through the hurting. the breaking. the healing. i don't think i could ever thank you enough. i love you.

to caroline-
thank you, for being the beautiful soul that you are. you introduced me to writing and i still remember the day i bought my first journal. i told you that i would fill it all up and publish my own book one day to share my art with the world. here i am today, doing so. you have taught me that my own company and my own love always comes first, before anyone else's. i have since then learned how to love myself. i will always be grateful for you. i love you.

to anyone who has supported my work. if i haven't thanked you enough. please know, i thank god for you every day.

to him,

thank you, for showing me
what love isn't.

لـه .

شكرا لك، لإظهار لـي
مـا الـحب لـيس.

for anyone who has been through the days where
you did not want the morning to begin nor the night to come to an end.

this is for you.

لـمن كـان خلال الأيـام الـتي
كـنت لا تـريـد الـصبـاح لـبدء ولا لـيـلة لـلوصول إلـى
نـهـايـته .

هذا لك.

"what is love?"

a question, frequently asked

think of love as
the stars and the night
how they cannot be divided

"ما هو الحب؟"

سؤال، كثيرا ما يطلب

التفكير في الحب
النجوم و الليل
كيف لا يمكن تقسيمها

euphoria,

do you know what it feels like?
because i do.
this moment, being right here with you.

1/19/16 3:13AM

الـنشوة ،

هل تـعرف مـا تـشعر بـه؟
لأنـني أفـعل.
هذه الـلحظة، ويـجري هـنا مـعك.

i watched him while he slept
my eyes were
heavy, half closed

but,

i couldn't sleep
i had to watch him
to appreciate him

so, i watched-
until the sun came up

only to look at him again
this time, with him looking back

—   *good morning*

tach.y.car.di.a

an abnormally rapid heart rate

–   when our hands meet

he walked in
while i sat on the floor
painting on a new canvas

he watched me for some time
before deciding to walk towards me
and ask,
"what are you pouring your heart
out on today?
for each one of your brush strokes
to be filled with such passion"

to which i replied,

"frida kahlo once said,
i paint flowers so they will not die"

he said,
"that's beautiful,
but what you are painting does not
look like any flower that i know of"

i smiled
i said to him,

"i know,
i am not painting flowers"

as he stood behind me
with my back pressing gently
against his legs
i lifted my head looking up to where
my eyes met his-

"i am painting our love"

i put his hand on my heart.
"this is how you make me feel,"
i said.

alive

أضع يده على قلبي.
"هذه هي الطريقة التي تجعلني أشعر"
انا قلت.

على قيد الحياة

his presence is bliss

وجوده هو النعيم

we live in a world where countries
are constantly at war with each other

but, somehow
i look at you
and i still find peace

نحن نعيش في عالم حيث البلدان
هي باستمرار في حالة حرب مع بعضها البعض

ولكن بطريقة أو بأخرى
أنا أنظر إليك
و ما زلت تجد السلام

8

thank you.

for being you.

1/9/16 3:21am

he handed me a rose and he said to me,
"i will love you
until the day
this rose will die"

knowing that-
                        love,
            real love,
our love,

won't ever die

even after colors fade and appearances change

as i walk down the narrow gallery
filled with art hung
parallel to each wall
taking my time to admire each piece

i reach the end of the hall
and i find you
standing,
not hung on the wall

but you are the most exquisite piece
i have ever seen
although they say art is not supposed
to be touched,

i want you to know-

you have touched me

my head,

        on his chest.

his heart beat

        always brought me to

serenity

    &

when i listened close enough,
i noticed our hearts would beat together as one

- in sync

i was once told that love never dies
if you fall in love
with their eyes

قـيـل لـي مـرة واحدة أن الـحب لا يـمـوت أبـدا
إذا كـنت تـقع فـي الـحب
مـع عـيـونـهم

we were never promised forever,
but we live our lives as if we were-

promised infinity
promised a lifetime

so, we give less and less each day

to our minds
to our souls
to our faith
to our lives
to the damn people that we love
because well do it *later* right?

> we are so stuck on later
> that we forgot about now

so, why not
why not choose today to give more?
to our minds
to our souls
to our faith
to our lives
to the damn people that we love

choose today to realize
we were never promised forever

06/24/16 10:33am

14

your love

fills me up

&

drowns me

all on the same day

i call this-

the sunrise & the sunset

حـبـك

يـمـلأنـي

و

يـغـرق لـي

كـل ذلـك فـي نـفـس الـيـوم

أدعو هذا-

شروق الـشمس ومجموعة الـشمس

you will have days where
you will fall apart
you will have days where
you won't feel whole

on these days,
i want you to
take a piece of yourself
and hold it up towards the light

tell me what you see
show me all the different variations of colors
that have put you together so beautifully

–   stained glass window

i still think it's incredible
how we have remedies
for pain

        (drugs, alcohol, lovers)

but,

what do i do

when the one causing my pain
is also my *remedy*?

every time our eyes meet,
i feel this rush of adrenaline.

i don't know if we are meant to be
or if it's just our memories...

في كل مرة تلتقي أعيننا،
أشعر هذا الاندفاع من الأدرينالين.

أنا لا أعرف ما إذا كان من المفترض أن يكون
أو إذا كانت مجرد ذكرياتنا...

how do you expect to have a relationship with someone
who doesn't have a relationship with their self?

كيف تتوقع أن يكون لديك علاقة مع شخص ما
الذي ليس له علاقة مع الذات؟

he was the reason
why i picked up a pen

i thought,

if i could write about
how i felt

people would be able to see
how beautiful
pain can be...

كـان الـسـبـب
لـمـاذا الـتـقـطت الـقـلم

اعتقـدت،

إذا كـنت يـمكن أن يـكتـب عن
كيف شعـرت

الـنـاس سوف تـكون قـادرة عـلى رؤيـة
كم هو جمـيـل
الألـم يـمكن أن يـكون...

& i guess i am content
with pain.

isn't it better to feel,
than to feel nothing at all?

& أعتقد أنا المحتوى
مع الألم .

أليس من الأفضل أن يشعر،
من أن يشعر شيئا على الإطلاق؟

a daily reminder:

love will never stay
where it truly deserves to be...

time will always tell

تذكير يوميا :

الحب لن يبقى من أي وقت مضى
حيث يستحق حقا أن يكون...

الوقت سوف اقول دائما

i miss him

the way he used to make me smile
the way he used to make me laugh

the way, he used to love me

although he is sitting

right here, beside me
hand in hand

i see us both as

two countries
next to each other,

but still
many miles apart

he looked at me with those eyes
- the type that consume you

he said to me, "you are a work of art,
one painted by either picasso or monet"

i smiled. curiously, i asked-

"why those two?
neither artist exists in this time"

to which he replied,
"because, my dear -your soul exists
in the wrong time and your heart
beats in the wrong era"

...and you would think that a masterpiece
painted by either picasso or monet

would be
admired, appreciated
in this day and time

but instead,
he took pieces of me
pieces of the masterpiece

for him to keep

i call him an antiquary

if he has never treated you the right way

he will never be able to love you-

the right way

إذا لم يعاملك بالطريقة الصحيحة
وقال انه لن تكون قادرة على الحب لك-
الطريق الصحيح

what does it all come down to
at the end of the day
when the sun sets
and the night starts to fall
wouldn't you say love?

is it not love that we always wish
we had given more of
or received more of?

sure,

he can give you the life you want…
but, what about love
can he give you
the love you want

09/02/16

26

your heart the strongest muscle in your body.
your heart is the strongest organ in your body.
it fights for you.

every. day.

but, your heart my dear
is also the softest place when it comes to pain.

you must now fight for your heart.

in return,
let it heal you.

قـلـبك هو أقـوى الـعضلات فـي جسمك.
قـلـبك هو أقـوى جهـاز فـي جسمك.
انـهـا تـحـارب بـالـنـسبة لـك.

كـل. يـوم.

ولـكن، قـلـبك يـا عزيـزي
هو أيـضا أنـعم مكـان عنـدمـا يـتعلق الأمـر الألـم.

فقـد حـان الـوقت لـلقـتـال مـن أجل قـلـبك.

فـى الـمقـابـل,
والـسمـاح لـهـا شفـاء لـك.

i asked her,

"do you know what it feels like to be in love
with two different people at the same time?"

she said, "no"

i replied,

"i do. i am in love with two different people,
the man i once knew and the man i now know"

"and what does it feel like?", she asked

i responded-

it feels like heaven and hell,
intertwined

28

tonight,

i miss you dearly
i will fall asleep with my hand on my chest
to stop my heart from hurting
to hold it from falling apart

yearning for your body next to mine,

even if only
i could have your hand in mine

الــليــلة ،

أنــا أفــتقــدك كـثيــرا
سوف تـغفـو مـع يــدي عـلى صدري
لــوقـف قــلبــي مـن الأذى
لإمـساكـها مـن الانـهيـار

الــتوق لــجسمك بـجانـب الألـغـام ،

حتـى لـو كـان ذلـك فـقط
يــمكـن أن يـكون يــدك فـي الــمـنجم

29

i was my own safe haven
i never needed saving
i was my own home
i never needed repairing

you came into my life
unexpected and turbulent
equivalent to a tsunami

i did not have the choice of
letting you in or not
i did not have the choice of
fighting back

you. took. everything.
everything, i ever had...

my love, *deprived*
scattered throughout
the pacific

the nails and bolts that once
held up the foundation of
my home have reached the
bottom of the ocean

i used to be my own
safe haven
& now, i don't even know
what safe means...

against all odds-
i am the one who needs saving

- refugee

you came into my life
broken
while i was whole

not that i am one who pushes the broken away –

if anything,
i am a shelter to them
they take from me until they become full
and then they get up and leave…

but, before you go-
i said to him

take a look at what you have done to me

do you see how you have left whole and i am left broken?
do you see how you have found strength in your love and
how you have left mine diluted?

if they bring out the worst in you,
don't you think they are the worst for you?

إذا كانت تبرز أسوأ فيكم ،
لا تعتقد أنها أسوأ بالنسبة لك؟

you have swept through me
like a wild fire
still alive
still burning
inside of me

you have tarnished all that
once held durability
every bone
every muscle

...& how could we forget about
the most durable of them all-
my heart

now, everything i touch
i destruct...

i wake up each morning
-late
almost every other day for work

i stay in bed that extra minute
any extra minute i can get

to get that little feeling of heaven again…
holding onto my comforter,
wishing it was you comforting me instead

i close my eyes and think about us
think about our memories

any
little memory
i can remember

how perfect it used to be…

because, at this time- right now
you would be lying next to me…

i open my eyes
and reach over to touch you

knowing you are not there

       .. my heart aches

every morning

nothing is perfect now
and all i have is our memories…

maybe,
it's time for me to get up
and get dressed for work

maybe,
it's time for reality.

mourning in the morning

03/30/16 8:37pm

the way that i have touched you

the next woman, she will know
that you have been loved before

a woman, similar to me
will be aware of men like you
who know nothing of love

but, you
my dear

you will surprise her with love she
has never seen nor felt before

from the way that i have touched you
from the way that i have loved you

- imprint

when i don't know what to write
i think i'm lost
with my heart and my mind

عندما لا أعرف ماذا أكتب
أعتقد أنني فقدت
مع قلبي و ذهني

certain people are brought into our lives- not to stay,
but to rather show us why they do not deserve to.

يتم جلب بعض الناس إلى حياتنا - وليس للبقاء،
ولكن بدلا من ذلك تبين لنا لماذا لا يستحقون.

i apologize if i am unable to love you
the right way

for,

i have never been loved
the right way

أعتذر إذا كنت غير قادر على الحب
الطريق الصحيح

إلى عن على،

لم أكن أبدا أحب
الطريق الصحيح

we are so focused on
counting the years we've spent together

we forget to love each other

ونحن نركز على ذلك
عد سنوات، قضينا معا

ننسى أن نحب بعضنا البعض

i reach out to you
as the ocean does for the shore

i reach out to you

but, you are too far to be grasped

too far to be held

too

                                        far

to be loved

my heart pours out for you, like

heavy
heavy rain

and my love flows through you, like

heavy
heavy wind

i am known as a monsoon, but i am not seasonal.

i am here to stay.

- permanent

you don't need to tell me what hurts

the sadness, in your eyes
speak for you

أنت لا تحتاج إلى أن تخبرني ما ألمك

الحزن، في عينيك
يتحدث لك

you must learn to walk away from men

whose eyes forbid to meet yours
when you speak

—   respect

يـجب أن تـتعلم الـمشي بـعيدا عن الـرجال

الـذيـن عيـونـهم سمح لـتلبية لـك
عـندمـا تـتكلم

- احتـرام

there will be times in our lives
where we will find people
who aren't whole, but instead
half-full and most of the time-

empty

when we are whole ourselves
we encounter these people
with everything to offer them

everything they have never had nor felt

or- at least, once had...

so, we give and we give
to make them whole

to see them smile
to see them happy

because we promised them love
we promised them everything

but, what we don't notice is that
we are giving to make one whole

as we are slowly becoming half-full,
empty

ourselves

–   the wrong kind of love
07/02/16 1:03AM

i cannot remember the day you left me.
maybe, it is because i had lost you long before that…

when you left,
you still had pieces of me in you

but, now i see

they weren't meant for you to keep
for i have found them left behind

for me to keep

thank you for returning what has
always belonged to me

how foolish are people to believe that
time determines when we are capable
of loving someone
or that it can determine the amount of
love we have for someone

days, months, years
do not determine love

have you not noticed?

when the ones we loved have left

we do not replay the years in our head,
we replay the moments in which
we fell in love each time

07/06/16

if you are any less happy
in their company than in your own

- leave

love should never drain you

إذا كنت أقل سعادة
في شركتهم من الخاصة بك

- غادر

الحب يجب أبدا استنزاف لك

people will settle for anything

anything that claims to love them

الـنـاس سوف تـسويـة لأي شـيء

أي شيء يـدعـي أن أحـبـهـم

you would have found thousands
of untold stories in his eyes

if you looked at him the way i did
if you knew him the way i did
if you read him the way i did

- *never let a man walk away from you*
as an unopened book

my heart was too heavy
for you to carry
my heart was filled with
too much love

for you to even understand
what the simplest form
of love was...

it's okay

i cannot blame you,
for your hands
weren't sturdy enough
for my heart

i cannot blame you
for not being able to understand
what was never given to you

i can only hope
for you to decide
to fill your heart with love
someday

...enough love to be able to
at least, love yourself

first

- *when you fall in love with the*
  broken ones...

you will know when they have left.

you will know,

when you come home to a house emptier
than yourself.

وسوف تـعرف مـتى غـادروا.

انـت سوف تـعلم،

عندمـا تـأتـي إلـى الـمنزل إلـى مـنزل إمـبتييـه
مـن نـفسك.

what we had was never love.
it was me trying to love you
& you, not allowing.

why did it take me so long to see

i was at war.

   with myself.

i am still learning

how

not to love you

- *the process of letting go*

انا لا ازال اتعلم

ماذا

لا أحبك

- عملية التخلي عن

55

he always came and left
as he pleased

i should have known men like him never stay.
i should have known men like him have no permanent home.

−   *nomad*

we were once, both

filled with love
overflowing with details

& now, all that is left of us

are outlines

of where our details used to lie

—   silhouettes

there are days where moments that
i have had with you

flood my mind

what if
i had done things differently or
said things differently

maybe, just maybe
you would still be here…

it took me a while
to realize that anything
i would have said or done differently
wouldn't have made you stay

Women like me

for the longest time, i was never able to understand why women wouldn't leave the toxic relationships they were in. until it happened to me. until, i too became a woman in that same position. the hardest part? leaving. for good. until we found our way back to each other again. similar to the way the night melts into the day. see, women like me don't let go because we feel the need to stay. to fight. to not give up. lovely woman, i am not writing this to give you the strength to leave. lovely woman, i want you to try, *until you've tried*. give, *until you've given*. fight, *until you've fought*. cry, *until you've cried*. love, *until you've loved*. go through it. the pain. feel it. all of it. until you can't anymore. until you have no choice but to leave.

> — *if you are wondering*
> *what it feels like*
> *to be free*

i think deep down in our hearts
we know when someone isn't right for us...
the first time we see them differently ...

with the way they speak to us
how they touch or hold us
how they treat or hurt us

deep down in our hearts we get this feeling of
unease, uncertainty

this feeling that we choose to ignore
and we decide to stay

we want love and we want to be loved
so, we choose to settle for any love
not knowing love isn't a settlement

when you see someone differently
they are showing you who they truly are

their raw self

... we become too blind to see it ourselves

& i cannot tell you that love is blind

because,

      real love
      true love

wouldn't make us blind
to what we are supposed to see...

- don't ignore that feeling

when people leave
we are quick to react with
anger and harsh words

when people leave-

let them

don't react with anger,
but rather peace

this is your closure,
you just don't know it yet

عندما يغادر الناس
نحن سريعة للرد مع
الغضب والكلمات القاسية

عندما يغادر الناس -

دعهم

لا تتفاعل مع الغضب،
بل السلام

هذا هو إغلاق الخاص بك،
كنت فقط لا أعرف ذلك حتى الآن

if there was one thing that i wish
my mother could have told me growing up...

sometimes,
your love is too much
& sometimes, people leave because of this.
they cannot handle your love-

        how much it is

           how strong it is

please don't ever think there is anything wrong
with you, your love or how much you love

because, one day you're going to find someone
and this person will be able to handle your love
because they need it
this person will be deserving of your love
because they want it

your love is too much, simply because

one day, all of this love is going to pour out of you
into someone else

someone who has been feeling empty for so long-

& my dear,
        you are going to fill them up

           because your love is too much

        and that will always be a good thing

what if we had met in another time,
would we have loved in another way?

ماذا لو التقينا في وقت آخر.
هل كنا نحب بطريقة أخرى؟

everyone deserves love
even the ones
who were incapable of

loving you

الـجميـع يـستـحق الـحب
حتى تـلك
الـذيـن كـانـوا غيـر قـادريـن عـلى

أحبك

you cannot speak poetry to those who do not
understand your language

    −   fluent

لا يـمكنك الـتحدث الـشعر لأولـئك الـذيـن لا
فـهم لـغـتك

- بـطلاقـة

have you ever seen the way the sun light
gleams through a tree
unveiling all of its beauty

the broken branches and the discolored leaves...

my love is like the sun
and you,
  my dear,
    you are like the tree

my love will shine through you and
i will expose every part of you to me,

your strongest branches and your weakest stems
each leaf filled with color and ones left colorless

and

when i am able to see all of you
know every detail
down to your roots

my love, the sun

will still shine towards you

the weight you carry
is not baggage

it is your strength

الـوزن الـذي تـحمـله
لـيـس الأمـتعة

فـمـن قـوتـك

for a friend,

you keep memories of her
on the tips of your fingers

i can tell,

by the way you bring light and happiness
to everything you touch

i see the way you form a fist and hold tightly
onto the pendant around your neck
where her face is engraved

i see the way you move your fist
close to your heart
& keep it there

because that it where you keep her...

and i am writing this to let you know,
that is where she keeps you too...

something good will find you,
if you let it.

     — patience

شيء جيد سوف تجد لك،
إذا كنت السماح لها.

     — الصبر

it is okay to love

and not have that love returned to you

this does not mean you are

not enough

for the ones who were

unable to love you

needed your love

more than you did

you have shown them selflessness

you have shown them love

you. are. more. than. enough.

  – abundant

فـمـن بـخـيـر أن الـحـب
ولـم يـكـن هذا الـحـب عـاد لـك
هذا لا يـعـنـي أنـك
لـيـس كـافـي
بـالـنـسـبـة لأولـئك الـذيـن كـانـوا
غيـر قـادر علـى الـحـب لـك
تـحـتـاج حبك
أكـثر مـمـا فـعـلـت

كـنت قـد أظهـرت لـهم الانـانـيـة
كـنت قـد أظهـرت لـهم الـحب

أنـت. لـ. أكـثر مـن. كـافـيـة.

  – الـوفـيـرة

70

i have never been in love
the way i imagined to be

but, i write about it all the time

لـم أكـن فـي الـحب
الـطريـقـة الـتي تـخيـلـت أن أكـون

ولـكن، أنـا أكـتب عن ذلـك فـي كـل وقت

71

& how could i ever forget you?
when every single memory of you
has been embedded inside my heart

وكيف يـمكن أن نـنسى لـك مـن أي وقت مضى؟
عندما ذكريـات كنت قـد تـم
جزء ا لا يـتجزأ مـن قـلبي

why is it that
when the sun shines toward us
we look the other way

or

when it rains
we stay inside
admiring the peace from afar

.. the love that we dream of having
reminds me of the sun and the rain

so, why

why do we look away
from the love that we know
will give us warmth

why do we hide away from
the love that we know
will bring us peace

why do we guard ourselves
of all things on this earth
that make us feel alive?

to my readers,

i want you to wake up each day and appreciate
the beauty around you
the life around you

do you ever get the chance to look at the sky and question why
it has a tint of red or orange today when yesterday it was blue?

these are the little things that matter
appreciate them

when it comes to love-

always take that chance
always take that risk

i know it's hard,
the thought of getting hurt again

go for it

choose love

from what i've learned,
what hurts us
only makes us stronger

so,

you will either find love

or

more strength

i came across an elderly man one day and he immediately
brought up his wife, when speaking to him.

in those few minutes he explained to me how he met her, how
beautiful she was, how long they have been together and how
he still knows the size of her waist.

after our conversation had come to an end, we said goodbye and
he walked away.

in that moment of us parting ways
i said to myself-

"*this is how you know when someone is in love with you,*
they tell strangers about you"

love that was given and not reciprocated to you
is not defined as wasted love

love can never be wasted

for you have given love
to one who needed it the most

how beautiful is it, that we exist?

كم هو جميل، أننا موجودون؟

i have traveled to all countries
and my soul still finds its way back to you

you must have always been a part of me

   –   home

لقد سافرت إلى جميع البلدان
وروحي لا تزال تجد طريقها إليك

يجب أن تكون دائما جزءا مني

–   منزل

don't you want to fall in love?

don't you want to fall so deep
in love

that the thought of being in love with someone
won't ever cross your mind

because you're already in it.

don't you?

there are many things in life that will make you feel

please make sure that you, yourself
are one of them

هناك العديد من الأشياء في الحياة التي سوف
تجعلك تشعر

تأكد من أنك نفسك
هي واحدة منهم

i want you to ask the one who loves you, if they love their self

now, tell me
if the one who claims to love you is confused by what you
have just asked
does this not make you wonder how they love you?

okay- maybe they don't understand
what you are asking

so, explain it to them. can you?

let me ask you this,
do you love yourself?

waiting to find happiness
will only leave you questioning
why you wasted so much time in the first place

happiness is here
happiness is now

في انتظار العثور على السعادة
سوف يترك لك فقط يتساءل
لماذا تضيع الكثير من الوقت في المقام الأول

السعادة هنا
السعادة إذا الآن

the idea of having a soul mate
has always been questioned

do they exist
or not?

well, i believe that you can fall in love
with anyone

but,

what you need to understand is-
every time you love

it will always be a different kind of love

        -you will never have the same love twice

so,

if soulmates do exist
and you do find the one

i imagine it to feel like,

every different kind of love
you have ever felt

combined as one

god has given us eyes
that bring us tears of pain
and tears of joy

the greatest blessing of them all

الله أعطانا عيون
التي تجلب لنا دموع الألم
والدموع من الفرح

أعظم نعمة من كل منهم

he took until there was nothing left
except for a hollow space of where my heart used to be

أخذ حتى لم يبق شيء
باستثنا، مساحة أجوف من حيث كان
قلبي

be like the sun,

give warmth
to those who only feel the bitter cold

give light
to those who only see the darkness

give, effortlessly

يــكون مــثل الــشمس،

وإعطاء الــدفء
إلــى أولــئك الــذيــن يــشعرون فــقط الــبرد القــارس

وإعطاء الــضوء
لأولــئك الــذيــن يــرون فــقط الــظلام

تــعطي، جــهد

am i hurt? yes.
but, i'll be okay.

do you know why?
because i told myself one day
to always choose love
even if it ends with pain.

i'll be okay.

how do you know when you have found the one?

your heart will know
& your mind won't question it

كـيف تـعرف عـندمـا كـنت وجـدت شخص صيح؟

قـلـبك سوف تـعرف
و عقـلك لـن تـشكك فـيـه

the rose you had given me
i still have it
-

years have passed
i kept it hoping you would return one day

today, i noticed that i have been holding onto
something that had died a long time ago...

our love

we live in a generation
where everything is done in a rush
as if we are running out of time

now, tell me-

if we are concerned about time
isn't this what our lives will consist of?
time?

eventually, everything we do will revolve around time

we rush to receive a degree in anything, to prove something
only to find out, we hate waking up for work each morning

we rush to succeed
only to find out, it is not about wealth

we rush to find happiness
only to find out, we have been looking for it in all the wrong
places

we rush to find love
only to find out, it has to be found within ourselves first

we rush to get married
only to end up wondering what it feels like to be in love

don't you see?
we are wasting time by rushing

by not doing what we really want to do..
how we really want to live..
how we really want to love..

my love is deeper than the five oceans combined

حبي أعمق من المحيطات الخمسة مجتمعة

a memory of someone you once loved
will always be the most meaningful souvenir
you will ever get to keep

ذاكرة لشخص كنت أحب مرة واحدة
وسوف يكون دائما تذكارية الأكثر وضوحا
سوف تحصل من أي وقت مضى للحفاظ على

i know your guard is up
but, real men weren't given
calloused palms
on their hands and feet

to not climb
the tallest mountains
and reach your love

your hands must have been designed
to fit perfectly into mine
because it feels like

i have known you
for a lifetime

يـجب أن تـكون قـد صممت يـديك
لـتناسب تـماما فـي الألـغـام
لأنـه يـشبـه

لـقـد عرفـتك
لـمدى الـحيـاة

maybe we'll find each other again
and we'll be able to begin
what had never begun

an everlasting love

ربما سنجد بعضنا البعض مرة أخرى
وسنكون قادرين على البدء
ما لم يبدأ

الحب الأبدي

wait
wait for that feeling

where he looks at you
& his whole world is

right there
in front of him

انـتظر
انـتظر لـهذا الـشعور

حيث يـنظر إلـيك
وعـالـمه كـله

هـنـاك
أمـامـه

why do you settle for an unadorned love
when you know there is a fire burning inside of you
for passion
for an extraordinary love

لـماذا تـسوية لـحب غير مـزين
عندما تـعرف أن هنـاك حريـق حرق داخل لك
لـلعـاطفـة
لـحب غيـر عـاديـة

i pray for the love you find one day to be mellifluous

— *sweetly flowing*

loving yourself

is

an everyday process
an everyday choice

Made in the USA
Middletown, DE
14 September 2017